THE 2001 NEW YORK YANKEES

SPORTS UNITE US

Published in the United States of America by Cherry Lake Publishing
Ann Arbor, Michigan
www.cherrylakepublishing.com

Reading Adviser: Marla Conn MS, Ed., Literacy specialist, Read-Ability, Inc.

Photo Credits: ©Ezra Shaw/Getty Images, 1; ©George Grantham Bain/Wikimedia, 5; ©Robert Mayer/
Sun-Sentinel/ZUMAPRESS.com/Newscom, 6; ©Robert Giroux/Getty Images, 9; ©Jonathan Daniel/
ALLSPORT/Getty Images, 10; ©Jed Jacobsohn/ALLSPORT/Getty Images, 13; ©Jed Jacobsohn/
ALLSPORT/Getty Images, 14; ©Ezra Shaw/ALLSPORT/Getty Images, 15; ©Al Bello/ALLSPORT/Getty
Images, 19; ©Doug Pensinger/Getty Images, 20; ©Ezra Shaw/Getty Images, 23; ©Doug Pensinger/
ALLSPORT/Getty Images, 24; ©Jeff Gross/ALLSPORT/Getty Images, 25; ©Al Bello/Getty Images, 28;
©Ezra Shaw/Getty Images, 29; ©Doug Pensinger/Getty Images, 30

Library of Congress Cataloging-in-Publication Data has been filed and is available at catalog.loc.gov

Cherry Lake Publishing would like to acknowledge the work of The Partnership for 21st Century
Learning.
Please visit *www.p21.org* for more information.

Printed in the United States of America
Corporate Graphics

ABOUT THE AUTHOR

J.E. Skinner received a Bachelor of Arts in Anthropology from Wake Forest University. She
loves writing both fiction and nonfiction books. In addition to reading as much as she can,
when J.E. isn't writing, she is hiking with her dogs and spending time with her family in the
beautiful outdoors.

TABLE OF CONTENTS

CHAPTER 1

The Team That Inspired a Nation

Baseball likely evolved from a British game called rounders. The main difference was that in rounders, the outfielders could hit the offense with the ball. Baseballs used to be soft. They were made from all kind of materials, from the soles of shoes to fish eyes! Baseball wasn't given official rules until 1846. The game didn't become a professional sport until after the Civil War ended in 1865.

Today, millions of boys and girls across 6 continents play Little League annually. Over 35 million people from 122 countries are **registered** baseball players. Around 18 million people watch the World Series each year. These seven games are played in the United States, and are the most popular games of the season. The best team wins the

The 1913 New York Yankees, just after they changed their name from the Highlanders.

World Series, and the players receive prize money and prestige. The 2016 World Series had a whopping 23 million viewers, who watched the Cubs win their first World Series since 1908!

One of the greatest baseball teams is the New York Yankees. They were originally called the Baltimore Orioles, and later the New York Highlanders. In 1913, they became the Yankees. With **legendary** players like Babe Ruth, Lou Gehrig, Joe DiMaggio, Whitey Ford, Yogi Berra, and Mickey Mantle, the Yankees appeared in every World Series from 1955 through 1964, except in 1959. They have won more World Series titles than any other team.

Yankees owner George Steinbrenner.

George Steinbrenner took over the team in 1973. The endless stream of money funneled into his team allowed Steinbrenner to **outbid** other teams for star players not under contract. This strategy for acquiring talent led many teams, and fans, to feel that the Yankees act dishonorably when signing their star players. For the 2001 season, the Yankees paid almost $110 million in salaries to their players. Because they hire the best players and win the most awards, many people outside of New York do not like the Yankees.

The Yankees ended their legendary 2001 season with 95 wins and 65 losses. It was their 99th season. Mariano Rivera, Derek Jeter, Roger Clemens, Bernie Williams, and Scott Brosius all starred on the team during the 2001 season. The Yankees played well as a team during both the regular season and their **postseason**. The Yankees finished their 2001 season as Division Champions. They lost the World Series 4–3 to the Arizona Diamondbacks. But by the end of the season, no one hated the Yankees. They had become America's favorite team.

Star Salaries

*The Yankees had four players in the top 30 highest salaries for the season. Their top two players, Derek Jeter and Bernie Williams, both made $12 million each. Pitchers Roger Clemens and Mike Mussina made about $10 million apiece. Newspapers and TV loved to talk about the best players. Many of these players were part of the Yankees. The Yankees made quite a bit of money in **advertisements**, and the players did, too.*

CHAPTER 2

Heartbreak

On September 11, 2001, two planes crashed into the World Trade Center in New York City. The North and South Towers caught fire. Within two hours of the attack, the North and South Towers **collapsed** and damaged ten other buildings in the area. It took eight months to clean up the site. A third plane crashed into the Pentagon. A fourth plane was headed towards Washington, D.C., but the passengers overtook the hijackers and crashed the plane in a field in Pennsylvania instead. The planes had been taken over by **terrorists**. Three thousand people died.

The United States was in shock. Americans couldn't believe that someone would hurt so many people on purpose. Within a few minutes of the planes hitting the buildings, firefighters, police

Terrorists crashed two planes into the World Trade Center North and South Towers on September 11, 2001.

officers, and rescue teams raced to the World Trade Center to help. Many rescue workers from other states went to New York to help. The news told sad stories about people getting hurt. Americans felt grief, but showed each other kindness and patience. Americans from all over the country helped however they could. Many people gave blood. Some sent money to the Red Cross and to other groups. Others took care of animals who had gotten lost in the smoke and mud. Businesses **unaffected** by the actual impact allowed strangers to charge their phones to call and reassure loved ones.

Fans hold up signs in support of their fellow Americans.

After the Twin Towers fell, Americans came up with a saying: "Never forget." They wanted to honor those who had died trying to save others. Americans hoped to come together and remember the people who intentionally put themselves in harm's way to protect American families. Some **charities** were set up to help family members. Others wanted to put a statue where the Towers fell. Some Americans wanted to rebuild the Towers. Another idea was to plant gardens where the Towers fell.

Americans also thought they should go back to their everyday lives. They wanted to seem strong, and to look like no one could upset them for too long. One of the ways they showed their strength and returned to normalcy was by watching baseball—America's favorite pastime. Americans also watched baseball because it took their minds off their sadness. Baseball was a way for people to join together in a common joy. The New York Yankees lived and played in New York. They became a symbol of hope and strength for New Yorkers, and for Americans.

A Quiet Week

The Commissioner of baseball is in charge of the money. Bud Selig was the Commissioner when 9/11 happened. Selig knew he would lose a lot of money if he canceled games. Out of respect, he canceled all the games until the next week. No one had ever pushed games back before. This caused games to be played in November. Until 2001, no baseball games had ever been played in November.

CHAPTER 3

A Return to Normalcy

After the attacks, Scott Brosius, the third basemen, said, "Is baseball really that important? Should we be playing again?" The Yankees didn't want to play a game when an entire nation was grieving. They didn't want to seem **disrespectful** to those who had lost, or couldn't contact, their loved ones. But it turned out that's exactly what Americans needed. They needed a break from their sadness, and they turned to the World Series.

The Yankees had won the World Series the last three years. Usually, baseball fans would want to see any team lose if they had won that many times in a row. But it was different after 9/11. Game 1 of the World Series started on October 27, and was played in Phoenix, Arizona. Despite the support for the

The Yankees show respect during the seventh inning stretch when the stadium begins singing "God Bless America."

Yankees, the team lost 9–1. Yankees fans told them not to worry, that they'd come back from behind, but the Yankees also lost Game 2. After two days of playing, the Yankees were already down two games to zero, with only five games left to play. The Yankees and Diamondbacks played Game 3 in Yankee Stadium. This was the first 2001 World Series game played in Yankee Stadium, and the fans went wild. Many Americans were rooting for the Yankees to win. Americans knew how much New Yorkers had struggled the past six weeks. The Yankees heard the fans

Jorge Posada of the New York Yankees hits a home run during Game 3 against the Arizona Diamondbacks.

chant "U-S-A, U-S-A!" in support of their fellow Americans. They wanted the Yankees to know that they weren't alone. The Yankees won Game 3 by a score of 2–1, and brought the Series to a 2–1 lead for the Diamondbacks.

Game 4 took place on Halloween. The game went into extra innings, and Derek Jeter walked up to the plate as the clock crept up to midnight. He hit a home run just after midnight, on the first of November! A World Series game had never been played past October. Jeter earned the name Mr. November. The Yankees won the game, and the next game after that.

Derek Jeter celebrates after scoring the winning home run during Game 4 against the Diamondbacks.

The Yankees thought they were on a roll. They had won three games in a row in New York, but they didn't win any more. The Diamondbacks came back from behind and won the World Series 4–3. Although the Yankees lost, Americans **bolstered** them, just as the Yankees lifted the nation's spirits. The 2001 World Series is thought to be one of the best World Series ever played.

The Perfect Strike

President Bush had the honor of throwing out the first pitch for Game 3. It was the first game of the 2001 World Series at Yankee Stadium. He had to put on a bulletproof vest under his FDNY fleece before he could walk out to the field. He passed Derek Jeter on his way to the field. Jeter told President Bush, "Don't bounce it. They'll boo ya." Bush threw a perfect strike. The crowd cheered so loudly that the ground shook.

Derek Jeter

This legendary shortstop is widely considered to be one of the greatest Yankees players of all time. "The Captain" played his entire career as a Yankee, and retired in 2014. The 1996 Rookie of the Year is attributed much of the Yankees' success in the 1990s and 2000s. One of his most popular plays was "The Flip" during Game 3 of the American League Division Series (ALDS). Jeter ran to the first baseline, catching a ball from the outfielder, Shane Spencer. "Captain Clutch" flipped it to the catcher, who tagged an A's player out. Experts say the play changed the **momentum** of the game, and the Yankees ended up winning the series. Jeter also formed the Turn 2 Foundation, which encourages children to "turn away from drugs and alcohol and 'TURN 2' healthy lifestyles."

CHAPTER 4

Healing a Nation

The team was in New York when the attacks occurred. Like their fellow Americans, they were shocked by the violence and terror surrounding the **tragedy**. They, too, were victims of the confusion and **trauma** that would plague New York—and the nation—in the upcoming months. Wanting to help, several Yankees went to rescue centers to give their support. They **comforted** families who had lost loved ones, or who didn't know where their families were. Many religions held services to support the families. The victims felt a sense of comfort to have the Yankees there. Some victims had been Yankees fans, and families were grateful for their presence. Bernie Williams, the Yankees' center fielder, walked up to a crying woman in the armory and

The Yankees wear hats in support of first responders.

told her, "I don't know what to say, but you look like you need a hug," and he hugged a complete stranger.

During the games, the Yankees wore hats that said FDNY for the New York Fire Department, and NYPD for the New York Police Department. The Yankees showed respect for the firefighters and police officers who risked their lives to save New Yorkers.

Billy Crystal is an actor and longtime Yankees fan. He saw that Americans were joining together to support the Yankees. He

The FDNY bears the American Flag during the National Anthem.

knew that most people didn't like the Yankees. He thought it was very respectful of others to know how much the Yankees were hurting. He also knew that the Yankees were taking on the duty of helping others through their sadness. During the 2001 World Series, Crystal said, "For the first time I think in the history of baseball, people around the country were pulling for the Yankees to win. This is a moment. Your politics go away."

The Yankees became America's heroes almost overnight. They took on the role of **boosting** Americans' spirits. They gave New Yorkers hope and a way to distract themselves when they were upset. The team was a balm for the deep wounds Americans felt. For months, the players worked **tirelessly** and shouldered the **tremendous** responsibility of lifting American morale. They played their hearts out during the World Series. They showed New Yorkers how to have strength and courage. The players showed Americans how to be brave and how to push through their sadness and anger. The Yankees were a symbol for hope and helped Americans tough it out and be strong.

Love for the Yankees

Americans from all over the country showed their support for New York and for the Yankees. The third basemen, Scott Brosius, remembers when the Yankees lost the first two games of a series against the Oakland Athletics. He said that fans called out to the team. They said they knew the Yankees would end up winning. Jorge Posada, the Yankees catcher, saw a huge sign in Chicago's stadium that said "Chicago loves New York."

CHAPTER 5

The Legacy

During each home game at Yankee Stadium, "God Bless America" plays in honor of those who died in 9/11. The former Yankees owner, George Steinbrenner, "wanted the song played to honor the nation, the service members, and those who fell on 9/11." This tradition has carried on ever since.

There are many statues and parks in honor of the victims of 9/11. Monument Park is one such park inside Yankee Stadium. It lists the names of great baseball players. On September 11, 2002, a section was added to remember the victims of 9/11. In 2009, Yankee Stadium moved across the street. Monument Park moved as well, and is still in the stadium. The **architects** designing Monument Park spent quite a bit of time planning to make sure the park was visible to those in the stadium. They added pearl

A wreath sits next to the 9/11 memorial honoring first responders in Monument Park.

blue granite from Finland to draw attention to the park. Yankee Stadium hosts many tours throughout the day, and many visitors also visit Monument Park in celebration of recognized players, and in respect for those who fell. At **Ground Zero**, there is a statue called "Horse Soldier," which depicts a Special Forces soldier riding into Afghanistan on a horse.

Many groups and programs were set up to help people who were hurt in 9/11. On September 11, 2016, the Yankees recognized the Fort Belvoir Wounded Warrior Care Center and the Walter Reed National Military Medical Center. These places gave hurt

Yankee fans go wild during Game 4 of the World Series.

military members a place to heal. Some programs work with children who lost family members. Other programs assist firefighters and police officers who were hurt helping the victims. Many of these groups have done research to help with **PTSD**. This disorder can happen to people dealing with trauma or abuse. Rescue and recovery workers tend to suffer from PTSD at far higher rates than people in less high-stress careers.

For seven days during the World Series, the Yankees took Americans' minds off their grief. The Yankees returned Americans to what their lives were like before the attack.

To honor the New York Fire Department, the Phoenix Fire Department raises the American flag during the first game of the World Series between the Yankees and the Diamondbacks.

Americans enjoyed a game that was "as common as apple pie." Both fans and players said there was a charge to the air when the Yankees played. Although they lost the World Series, many Yankees fans said they didn't really care. What healed them the most wasn't winning a baseball game. What healed them was Americans showing their strength by uniting as a nation.

"They Were Going Up"

Firefighters and police officers arrived at the World Trade Center within a few minutes of the attack. They immediately ran inside the building to save as many people as they could. The speech writer for Mayor Giuliani, John Avlon, talked about how the firefighters and police officers climbed the stairs of burning buildings while others were escaping. Avlon said, "This was the image that survivors would repeat over and over, 'as we were going down, they were going up.'"

Tuesday's Children

This program was established during 9/11 and its aftermath. It was designed to mentor children who have lost loved ones to terrorism or other violence. Tuesday's Children has a long-term approach to therapeutic care. Resilience-building services help children learn to cope and strategize working through trauma. Counseling is offered through the program for children and their families. Tuesday's Children also helps children and adults thrive through outreach programs. Trauma survivors take comfort in the social support of other families in the community. Sharing similar stories anchors and empowers survivors. In 2011, several children who had lost family members met with Yankees players who reached out to show their support. Derek Jeter attended the meet-and-greet, delighting young fans and giving them hope.

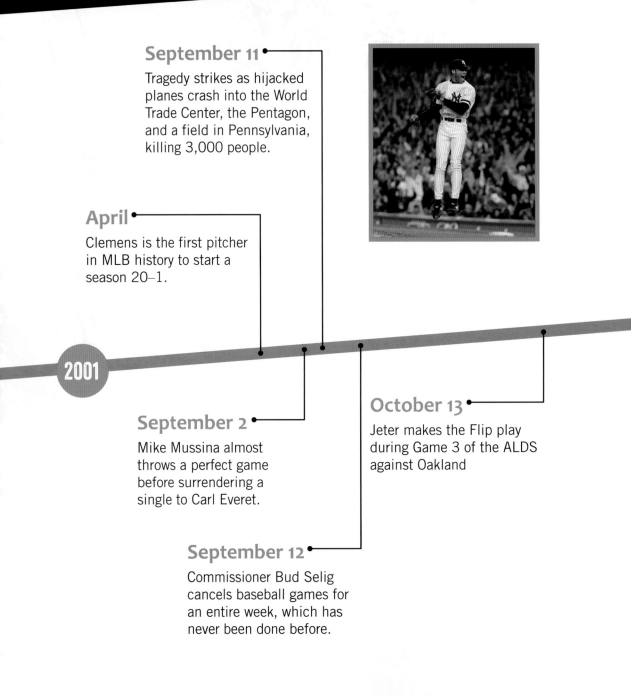

September 11

Tragedy strikes as hijacked planes crash into the World Trade Center, the Pentagon, and a field in Pennsylvania, killing 3,000 people.

April

Clemens is the first pitcher in MLB history to start a season 20–1.

2001

September 2

Mike Mussina almost throws a perfect game before surrendering a single to Carl Everet.

October 13

Jeter makes the Flip play during Game 3 of the ALDS against Oakland

September 12

Commissioner Bud Selig cancels baseball games for an entire week, which has never been done before.

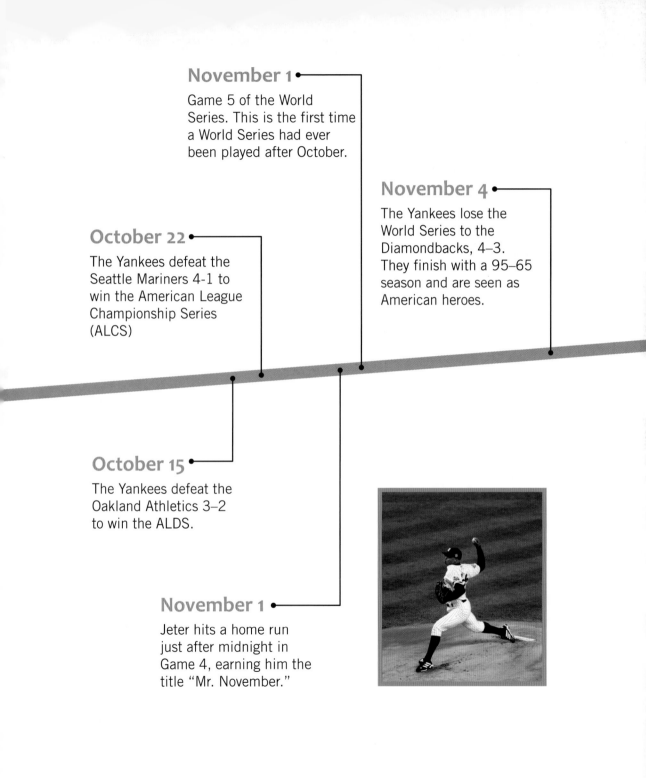

November 1

Game 5 of the World Series. This is the first time a World Series had ever been played after October.

November 4

The Yankees lose the World Series to the Diamondbacks, 4–3. They finish with a 95–65 season and are seen as American heroes.

October 22

The Yankees defeat the Seattle Mariners 4-1 to win the American League Championship Series (ALCS)

October 15

The Yankees defeat the Oakland Athletics 3–2 to win the ALDS.

November 1

Jeter hits a home run just after midnight in Game 4, earning him the title "Mr. November."

Think About It

Think of games you've watched or have been to. Have you ever seen emergency personnel on the field when they weren't providing medical services? What is important about first responders taking the field at a World Series game after 9/11?

What do you think it meant for fans to sing the National Anthem while watching the New York Fire Department honor the flag and the United States?

What do you think being at Yankee Stadium meant for the New York Fire Department?

How do you think 9/11 affected emergency personnel both in New York and the rest of the United States?

Learn More

BOOKS

Baskin, Nora Raleigh. *Nine, Ten: A September 11 Story*. New York: Atheneum Books for Young Readers, 2016.

Euchner, Charles C. *The Last Nine Innings: Inside the Real Game the Fans Never See*. Naperville, IL: Sourcebooks, 2006.

Stout, Glenn. *The New York Yankees*. New York: Little, Brown, 2008.

ON THE WEB

9/11 Memorial & Museum Website
https://www.911memorial.org

History.com
http://www.history.com/news/category/baseball

Official New York Yankees Website
https://www.mlb.com/yankees

GLOSSARY

advertisements (AD-vur-tyze-mints) things that are shown to the public to help sell a product

architects (AR-kih-tekts) people who design buildings

bolster (BOHL-stur) to support and encourage

boosting (BOOS-ting) lifting or raising

charities (CHER-ih-teez) actions or donations that help the poor, ill, or helpless

collapse (kuh-LAPS) to break down completely

comfort (KUHM-furt) to soothe or support

disrespectful (dis-ri-SPEKT-ful) showing a lack of regard for

Ground Zero (GROUND ZEER-oh) the World Trade Center site, after 9/11

legendary (LEH-juhn-der-ee) very famous because of special qualities or abilities

momentum (moh-MEN-tuhm) driving power or strength

outbid (owt-BID) to offer more money on

postseason (POST-see-zun) a period of time right after the regular season when teams compete in a series of games to determine a champion

PTSD (PEE-TEE-ESS-DEE) short for post traumatic stress disorder; a mental condition that some people have after a traumatic event

registered (REH-juh-sturd) officially recorded

terrorists (TEHR-ur-ists) people who commit violence against a person or another country

tirelessly (TAI-ur-lis-lee) never getting tired

tragedy (TRA-jih-dee) a dreadful or fatal event

trauma (TRAH-muh) a very difficult experience that causes someone to have mental or emotional problems, usually for a long time

tremendous (truh-MEN-dis) extraordinary in excellence or size

unaffected (uhn-uh-FEK-tid) not influenced or changed

INDEX